BREAKING FREE

A Guide to Overcome Limiting Beliefs and Thrive in Life

FARHAN KARDAME

INDIA • SINGAPORE • MALAYSIA

Copyright © Farhan Kardame 2024
All Rights Reserved.

ISBN 979-8-89233-588-1

This book has been published with all efforts taken to make the material error-free after the consent of the author. However, the author and the publisher do not assume and hereby disclaim any liability to any party for any loss, damage, or disruption caused by errors or omissions, whether such errors or omissions result from negligence, accident, or any other cause.

While every effort has been made to avoid any mistake or omission, this publication is being sold on the condition and understanding that neither the author nor the publishers or printers would be liable in any manner to any person by reason of any mistake or omission in this publication or for any action taken or omitted to be taken or advice rendered or accepted on the basis of this work. For any defect in printing or binding the publishers will be liable only to replace the defective copy by another copy of this work then available.

Contents

Acknowledgement

All praise and thanks to Allah for planting the seeds of writing this book and guiding me to nourish and harvest it.

I dedicate this book to my late father and my mother for instilling in me the strong values and principles that have made me the person that I am today.

A special thank you to my wife, for being my biggest fan and always being the pillar of support as I pursue my crazy dreams.

To my 4 daughters, my princesses, thank you for bearing with me during my writing journey and always motivating me every day.

Thank you to my brothers and my sister for always staunchly supporting me.

I am grateful to my mentors Arfeen Khan and Irfan Noorani for their guidance and support in my writing journey.

Thank you to my friend Anwar for always encouraging me and showing me my strengths.

Thank you to all the coaches from the Incredible You Mastermind who keep encouraging me in my pursuit of greater heights in my life.

And finally, thank you to all my extended family members, friends, and well-wishers who were directly or indirectly associated with me in the journey of writing this book.

Introduction

In the quiet moments when the world stands still, we often catch a glimpse of the immense potential that lies within us. Yet, for most of us, these moments remain fleeting, overshadowed by the cacophony of daily life, responsibilities, and the relentless pursuit of survival. We move through life with our heads down, our gaze fixed only on the path immediately before us, never pausing to look up at the vast horizon.

But it does not have to be this way.

In this book, "Breaking Free: A Guide to Overcome Limiting Beliefs and Thrive in Life," I invite you on a journey—a journey of self-discovery, transformation, and boundless growth. My purpose in authoring this book is simple yet profound: To help you realize the incredible potential within you and guide you towards harnessing it, not just for surviving but for thriving.

If you are reading this, chances are you are caught in the whirlwind of corporate life. Your days are a blur of meetings, deadlines, and obligations. You might even feel like you are living on autopilot, going through the motions without considering the bigger picture.

Let me assure you that you are not alone. This book is born from a similar experience. In 2017, after working as a finance and accounting professional for more than 15 years, I found myself out of a job, unable to secure a new one. It was a daunting time, but little did I know that it would mark the beginning of a remarkable journey that would lead me to write this book.

During this challenging period, I realized something that had eluded me for years. I constantly complained about not having enough time while working at a corporate job. But now, stripped of my job and its daily demands, I had no excuse. It was an awakening—a stark realization that the lack of time had never been the issue; it was how I chose to spend my time.

I seized this opportunity to spend time with myself, introspect, and reflect on my life. What I discovered was both profound and unsettling. My life lacked structure. I was merely a passenger, drifting through the currents of existence. Each day, I followed the same uninspiring routine—wake up, go to work, get stressed at work, return home, eat, watch TV, and engage in various activities, only to repeat the cycle endlessly. Time passed by unnoticed. Meanwhile, my children were growing up, and I failed to appreciate time's passage fully.

As I looked around, I saw a pattern that resonated with many around me. We were all trapped in a monotonous cycle. Life was slipping by, and it was time for a change. It was time for me to change.

My wake-up call extended beyond just my daily routine. I looked back at a time when I had been prescribed medication to manage my blood pressure. I resisted starting the medication initially, fearing it would become a lifelong commitment. My doctor offered a lifeline, challenging me to change my lifestyle—eat healthily, exercise, prioritize sleep, drink sufficient water, and maintain regular mealtimes. I tried to adhere to these changes initially, but sustaining them consistently proved challenging.

This cycle of resistance and relapse repeated itself until my doctor's stern warning: "You are risking your life." Eventually, I started to take medication to manage my blood pressure.

Remarkably, I, who had never read fiction or nonfiction books before, developed a newfound love for nonfiction literature. One of the books I read stood out: "The Magic of Thinking Big" by David Schwartz. It offered valuable insights and guidance, particularly on the importance of public speaking and personal growth.

The book recommended joining Toastmasters to improve public speaking skills, and that advice struck a chord with me. In 2018, I took the plunge and became a Toastmaster. I gradually improved my public speaking skills by attending meetings, delivering speeches, and challenging my comfort zone. In the same year, I mustered the courage to participate in the club contest—a monumental achievement for someone who had once been shy and reserved.

Though I received encouraging feedback on my contest speech, one piece of advice left a lasting mark. It was clear that my speech had potential, but I had not sought guidance from a mentor. Determined to excel, I committed to collaborating with mentors for the 2019 club contest.

With the support of dedicated mentors, I clinched victory in both the International Speech and Humorous Speech categories, earning my spot in the area-level contest. I became the runner-up in the international speech category at the area level, allowing me to compete at the division level.

One of my most significant morale boosters was a surprising invitation—to serve as the emcee at my nephew's wedding. Many of my relatives were taken aback, as I was known to be quiet and reserved. Nevertheless, I embraced the role and received heartfelt praise for my performance.

Shortly after that, the president of our local community welfare organization approached me with a unique request—to conduct a quiz competition at their upcoming annual event. I embraced this opportunity wholeheartedly and executed the quiz competition with excellence.

As I witnessed this transformation in myself, I realized that my life had been profoundly impacted by acting upon the advice in a book. "The Magic of Thinking Big," published in 1959, had crossed my path in 2018, more than three decades after the author's passing away. It had empowered me to become a confident public speaker and had catalyzed remarkable change in my life.

This realization fueled my decision to write "Breaking Free." The profound impact of words on pages, even after the author departed this world, catalyzed this endeavor.

Looking back at my journey, I realized that I had been living in survival mode before facing these adversities, focusing solely on meeting basic needs. However, recent experiences showed me that my untapped potential had remained dormant for too long. With added effort and proactive measures, I gradually transitioned from mere survival to thriving.

My life had undergone a significant shift.

Now, I am sharing these insights with you, the reader. I have poured my sincere efforts into writing this book. I hope you find inspiration within these pages—an awakening to your potential. By reading this book, you will discover the keys to transcending survival mode and embracing a life in which you are thriving.

"Breaking Free" is more than a book; it is a testament to the transformative power of personal growth, and I wish it becomes a catalyst for positive change in your life. I hope this book will help to empower you with the tools and knowledge needed to reach your full potential.

I am also learning as I move forward in my life. Learning must continue till we breathe our last.

As you read this book, you will realize that all the transformations I have had, started when I reflected upon my life and gave it a deep thought. This process helped me in making progress in my life journey.

I have shared my stories from various times and areas of my life. I have also shared a few stories of people I was inspired by.

I do believe there is no one success formula for everyone. I request that whatever resonates with you and connects with you be refined to fit whichever area of your life you deem required.

Another point I want to make is that do not read this book in a hurry just for the sake of reading it. Take a pause when you feel a profound message coming towards you, highlight it, and do some reflection. Self-introspection is an integral part of Transformation.

To help you, I have given a small exercise at the end of every chapter to help you get some breakthroughs in your life. I request you to complete the exercise before you proceed to the next chapter. Some questions could be hard-hitting, but remember that something special that improves life is hidden in those essential tasks you may avoid. I want this book to be your guide—a reflective and informative companion on the journey ahead.

Welcome to an awakening and breaking free.

Declaration – Some content in the book is taken from multiple online sources. All the survey and research reports are taken from authentic sources. The personal stories of renowned figures are taken from news media and their videos on YouTube. I declare that all information is accurate to my knowledge.

Chapter 1

Trapped in the Rat Race

> *"The trouble with being in the rat race is that even if you win, you are still a rat."*
>
> ***– Lily Tomlin.***

The rat race is a term used to describe the competitive and stressful nature of modern life, where people constantly strive to achieve more.

Since childhood, most of us are handed a well-trodden map to success: study diligently, secure good grades, obtain a degree, and you are promised a prosperous future. It is a path ingrained in us from an early age, but it comes with a stark reality—few of us are taught how to face life's inevitable challenges, and financial literacy remains a neglected topic.

Personal Journey

My journey through this maze of expectations and societal norms began like many others. After tenth grade, I found myself standing at the crossroads, uncertain about my future. Yet, driven by the prevailing norms of society, I opted for the science stream. The eventual goal was to pursue engineering.

By the time my twelfth-grade results arrived, life had a different plan in store for me. I faced the harsh truth of failure in one subject. I had two choices: retake the single subject for a passing grade or retake all the exams, offering a chance for a better result. Succumbing to societal expectations once again, I chose the path of reexamination for all subjects, sacrificing immediate success for a chance at a better outcome.

The second attempt proved successful in passing, but my grades remained average. Consequently, I was unable to secure admission to an engineering college. Destiny had other plans for me, nudging me toward the commerce stream.

My journey through higher education was far from smooth sailing. In my final year of BCom, fate dealt another blow—I failed a subject. As I had done in twelfth grade, I decided to retake all the exams. This time, I emerged with flying colors, earning a first-class degree.

With a bachelor's degree in commerce, I entered the corporate world as an accountant. The word "closing" is a frequently used term in the vocabulary of accounting professionals. Every month, we had to cope with the relentless task of closing financial statements, often sacrificing work-life balance to meet strict deadlines.

Fear was another everyday companion in the corporate realm. Many employees lived in constant worry of losing their jobs. Anxiety trickled down from bosses who, dealing with their job insecurities, inadvertently instilled fear in their subordinates. "Mistakes are not tolerated" and "Meeting the deadlines is paramount" were the mantras echoing through the office.

Most, if not all, employees were constantly worried about the urgent need to pay bills and meet immediate demands. Consequently, there was little focus on long-term goals and personal aspirations.

The fear of unemployment weighed heavily on individuals, locking them into the same job year after year. The fear of the unknown and the comfort of familiarity kept them rooted in their roles. Many resorted to the murky waters of office politics to secure their positions.

In my case, the corporate environment coaxed me toward this treacherous path. Yet, the principles of honesty and integrity I held dear prevented me from succumbing to the allure of politics. Instead, my ethical compass guided me towards a different route to impress my superiors—the pursuit of further education in the field of accounting.

Thus, my pursuit of the Management Accounting Certification (CMA) started. As I began this new journey, I realized it was far from a straightforward path. Multiple failures punctuated my quest for success. Achieving this coveted certification took six long years of persistence and resilience.

As I found myself jobless, reflecting on my life's journey, I could not help but draw profound insights from my educational experiences. I realized that much of what I had pursued in terms of education was merely a conformity to societal norms. However, amidst the struggles, a glimmer of positivity shone through—I had developed the character traits of perseverance and resilience.

My educational journey mirrors the broader rat race, trapping countless individuals. It often begins with well-intentioned expectations but can lead to feelings of entrapment and stagnation.

“

What about the rat race in the first place? Is it worthwhile? Or are you just buying into someone else’s definition of success? Only you can decide that, and you will have to decide it over and over and over. But if you think it is a rat race, before you drop out, take a deep breath. Maybe you picked the wrong job. Try again. And then try again.

— **Sheryl Sandberg.**

”

The Importance of Financial Literacy:

Amidst the challenges of the rat race, one often overlooked aspect that can significantly impact an individual's journey is financial literacy. Understanding and managing one's finances is a crucial skill that can empower individuals to make informed decisions about their money.

In my own experience navigating the corporate landscape, I realized that the lack of financial literacy was a pervasive issue. Despite their dedication and hard work, many employees struggled with financial stress. The absence of knowledge about budgeting, investing, and long-term financial planning contributed to the perpetual cycle of living paycheck to paycheck.

Financial literacy is not just about making money but about understanding how to make money work for you. It involves grasping concepts like budgeting, saving, investing, and debt management. Incorporating financial education into our academic and professional journeys can be a transformative step toward breaking free from the constraints of the rat race.

As we explore the multifaceted challenges of the modern pursuit of success, let us not overlook the profound impact financial literacy can have on our overall well-being.

A Global Phenomenon

My journey through the corridors of academia and the corporate world has offered me a glimpse into the very heart of the rat race. Yet, it is not a solitary experience. My story reflects a broader phenomenon that countless individuals struggle with daily. As I cast my gaze beyond the confines of my narrative, a staggering truth emerges—many people worldwide find themselves living lives that lack fulfillment and purpose, trapped in the relentless race.

Every year, we come across various surveys and research reports that paint a stark picture of the modern human condition, revealing the toll the rat race takes on our overall well-being.

Job Dissatisfaction and Loss of Purpose:

Numerous studies have shown a pervasive sense of job dissatisfaction and a loss of purpose among individuals in the workforce. A recent Gallup report (State of the Global Workplace: 2023) revealed that only 23% of employees feel engaged in their jobs. The majority, a staggering 59%, is reported to have a sense of disengagement, while another 18% have been described as "actively disengaged." This paints a disheartening picture of individuals simply going through the motions, lacking fulfillment in their work.

The employees go to work and watch the clock tick by without putting substantial effort into the workplace. Even with the minimum productivity, they are more likely to burn out due to the disconnection from the workplace. Gradually, the employees become actively disengaged, consequently losing their mental peace.

Furthermore, Deloitte's 2019 Global Human Capital Trends survey found that a significant percentage of millennials expressed a desire for work that has meaning beyond financial compensation. It is clear that for many, the pursuit of a paycheck is not enough. The absence of purpose in their professional lives has far-reaching consequences for their well-being.

Impact on Physical Health:

The relentless demands of the rat race have profound implications for physical health. It is no surprise that conditions like obesity, heart disease, and hypertension are on the rise. The sedentary lifestyle that often accompanies long working hours and the stress associated with pursuing success can take a toll on the body.

A 2018 study published in the Journal of Occupational and Environmental Medicine linked long working hours and high job demands to an increased risk of cardiovascular diseases. The physical well-being of individuals is compromised as they struggle with the pressures of corporate life, sacrificing exercise, proper nutrition, and adequate sleep.

Impact on Mental Health:

Several research reports paint a sad picture of a world where countless individuals are caught in the swirl of the rat race, their lives marked by dissatisfaction, stress, and a profound sense of unfulfillment. It is a reality that transcends borders, affecting people from all levels of society.

As I share my journey and these eye-opening statistics, it becomes clear that the rat race is not just a personal struggle but a collective experience, a societal phenomenon.

The rat race is a formidable force affecting individuals globally. As we navigate through personal narratives and statistical insights, it is evident that the quest for fulfillment and purpose is a universal pursuit. Moving forward, we will dive deeper into other painful areas and explore pathways to liberation.

Exercise

Self-Introspection:

Take a moment to ponder your current life circumstances. Do you find yourself entangled in the relentless pace of the rat race? Acknowledge your feelings and thoughts honestly.

Identifying Detrimental Activities:

If you answer yes, list specific activities or commitments contributing to your sense of being trapped. These could be professional, personal, or even habitual. Be as clear as possible.

Elimination Strategy:

For each identified activity contributing to the rat race, brainstorm actionable steps for elimination. Consider practical and realistic measures to free yourself from these burdens.

Cultivating Purposeful Activities:

Now, shift your focus to positive changes. What activities could you incorporate into your life to infuse it with more purpose and satisfaction? Think beyond the immediate demands and explore endeavors that align with your values and aspirations.

Remember, this exercise is a personal exploration with no right or wrong answers. It is a tool for self-discovery and a catalyst for positive change. Embrace the process and envision the transformation that awaits.

Chapter 2

Poor Habits

> *"To change a habit, make a conscious decision, then act out the new behavior."*
>
> **– *Maxwell Maltz.***

For the ordinary person, the hustle and bustle of daily life often keeps them trapped in a vicious cycle of going through the motions. As they navigate through these motions unconsciously, many poor habits are developed along the way. These poor habits, often silent culprits, can hold us back from becoming the best version of ourselves.

Let me share some of the poor habits that had seeped into my life. After speaking to individuals from various walks of life, I have discovered a common thread that ties many of us together. These poor habits are prevalent among many people. While not all these habits were part of my own life, I have observed their presence in the lives of countless others.

Lack of Time Management

As I mentioned earlier, during my years of professional work, one of my most frequent complaints was not having enough time. Reflecting on those years, I realized that I seldom planned my days, which led to a sense of drifting with the tide. It is a paradox: everyone has the same 24 hours a day, yet many complain about not having enough time to accomplish their desires. Conversely, some individuals manage to achieve a great deal in their lives. Through my own experiences, I discovered that very few individuals take the time to analyze how they are spending their time and fail to work on optimizing it.

Abraham Lincoln once said, "Give me six hours to chop down a tree, and I will spend the first four hours sharpening the axe." Lincoln's wisdom teaches us that approaching a project or task is not about mindlessly working on it but planning how to complete it efficiently and effectively.

Most people struggle with time optimization because they have not established clear priorities. In my early years of professional life, my primary concern was completing tasks at work and meeting deadlines. Unfortunately, I neglected to consider how my time with family was spent. It was, subconsciously, not a priority for me. If I had recognized its importance and made it a priority, I would have undoubtedly allocated time for it.

Another challenge I faced, which is common among many people, is getting pulled away by distractions. These distractions can take various forms, such as a colleague or friend inviting us to chat casually or the constant notifications on our mobile phones, which have significantly disrupted our daily lives. Many smartphone apps distract us from our tasks, causing us to lose focus.

As we fail to set clear priorities and succumb to distractions, we often find ourselves pressed for time and resort to multitasking. However, multitasking may not be the productivity booster we believe it to be, as our brains cannot effectively focus on two tasks simultaneously. That is why, for effective time management, it is vital to establish priorities and adhere to them diligently without being swayed by distractions.

Lack of Self-Care

In 2014, something unsettling happened to me. I was in my office when I suddenly felt my heart racing. I was overwhelmed by the Palpitations that I had never experienced before. My ears grew unbearably warm, and I sensed something unusual happening in my head. It is hard to explain what exactly was happening, but I knew that something was awry with my health. I realized that I needed to see a doctor.

I told my boss I was not feeling well and needed to visit the doctor. As I entered the medical center, the first thing the doctor did was check my blood pressure. It was alarmingly high. Although the exact numbers elude my memory, it was around 165/100. It was my first experience. The doctor asked me about my sleep patterns, meals, and exercise routine. I could not recall my responses clearly, but it was apparent that I lacked adequate sleep and had an erratic meal schedule. My water intake was insufficient. The doctor's diagnosis was precise – I needed to take better care of myself.

The doctor inquired about physical exercise, to which my response was disheartening. I explained that my daily routine usually consisted of going from work to home, leaving little time for workouts. The doctor pronounced my lifestyle sedentary and recommended, at the very least, incorporating a half-hour daily walk, having meals at regular intervals, and ensuring adequate sleep. He emphasized understanding my body's sleep needs, ensuring I felt refreshed each morning. If my body requires 7 to 8 hours of sleep, I should prioritize it. If the body demands six hours, ensure that minimum amount. He said, "Your health is non-negotiable."

I gave it a shot following the doctor's instructions, but inconsistency crept back in due to a lack of commitment. Work stress perpetually loomed, with tight deadlines often forcing me to skip meals and neglect my water intake.

Approximately three months later, a familiar feeling returned, and it was even more severe. My boss insisted on accompanying me to the hospital this time. The doctor diagnosed my blood pressure at a staggering 195/110. I was put on bed rest. After an hour, my blood pressure had slightly improved but was still high. Once again, the doctor underlined the need for self-care.

I decided to heed this advice more seriously. I began walking regularly and adjusted my diet, reducing my junk food intake. My commitment lasted for a while, but then I returned to the autopilot mode of life.

After one more alarming incident, my doctor reached a breaking point, insisting that I take medication for my safety. He expressed concern about the potential effects on my organs and cautioned against further risks.

Reflecting on these incidents, I realized that we unconsciously drift with the tide when we fail to prioritize self-care and our daily activities. For many working professionals, the fear of job loss and the pressure to pay bills and provide for their families takes precedence. Our primary focus tends to be on our jobs because we need that paycheck at the end of the month, so we will do whatever it takes to secure it.

However, this singular focus often leads to neglect of other essential aspects of life, such as our health, family, and personal growth. When I contemplated these points, I understood that our life's wheel comprises several crucial components, and neglecting any one of them can negatively impact our entire existence.

Today, I am determined to transform myself. It has been six years since I started taking blood pressure medication, but my goal is to be medication-free within the next 6 to 12 months. Prioritizing my health, I have established a regular exercise routine and adhere strictly to a well-balanced diet. Self-care has become my top priority, and I am resolute in reversing my medical condition.

Just like me, thousands of people around the world have to face health issues due to a lack of self-care. But it does not have to be that way. In today's world, where we have access to any information we want on the internet, every individual needs to take responsibility for holistically caring for themselves. One must not wait for a health crisis to hit them. Proactive steps taken toward living a healthy lifestyle bring about a positive impact on the one who practices it.

Poor Money Spending Habits

If we look around us, most people, if not all, want more money, irrespective of their current financial status. In the race to have more money, these people sacrifice their well-being. Unfortunately, most of these people cannot properly manage the money they make. They can be more content if they plan their expenditure and spend their cash meticulously.

The most common bad habit related to managing money is failure to budget expenditures. Lack of budgeting monthly income and spending leads to unplanned and impulsive purchases that are usually unnecessary.

Even though I come from a finance background, I never had a monthly budget for expenses. Thankfully, I had the habit of thinking hard before spending my money, due to which my impulsive buying was not much. This helped me save money, but I never had the financial literacy to make sound investments.

Additionally, no savings are planned for investment and emergencies due to the absence of a budget. Although I used to save some money, it was never planned or organized.

Nowadays, banks worldwide encourage using credit cards, and most people fall for this trap. These people generally spend unconsciously by using credit cards. People rely on credit cards for spending as they offer convenience during purchases. Unfortunately, many of these people struggle later to clear the monthly balance. Eventually, it leads to high interest charges and debt accumulation.

Thankfully, I have been fortunate not to be lured by the glitter of Credit cards.

In the next chapter, I will share more poor money-spending habits and how they seep into our lives.

“Do not save what is left after spending, but spend what is left after saving.”

— **Warren Buffet.**

Instant Gratification

The advancement of the human race has made many products and services available instantly. It was only 35 to 40 years back that we saw a time when speaking regularly to our near and dear ones was challenging. Living far away or in another country, communication over the phone was not easily accessible or cheap. With modern technology, we can make video calls to almost any part of the world and not only manage to speak but also see them on the screen.

As we see advancement in technology, products are made available at the tips of the fingers. These products are delivered to our doorstep within a short time. Such services have reduced the patience threshold such that people expect everything to happen quickly.

Unfortunately, this does not work for most of the natural processes. If an individual must build strength, consistent workouts over a long time will give results. As people do not see results coming fast, they quit. Any significant change and development a person wants requires patience. Thus, a lack of patience hampers personal growth.

The above examples of poor habits are some that have created obstacles in the path towards making progress in our lives. That is why people get stagnant and fail to make much progress in their lives. I will share some strategies to overcome these problems as we move forward.

Please do the exercise on the next page before we move ahead to the next chapter.

Exercise

Self-Introspection:

Write down all the poor habits that have seeped into your life.

Identifying the consequences:

Try to understand which habits are causing the biggest hindrance in your personal and professional development.

Ratings:

Rate them based on priority to be eliminated or reduced.

Chapter 3

Trapped in Comparisons

> *"Everybody is a genius. But if you judge a fish by its ability to climb a tree, it will live its whole life believing that it is stupid."*
>
> **– *Albert Einstein.***

Albert Einstein's profound words resonate as we look into the intricate web of comparisons in which we often find ourselves entangled. From the initial stages of our lives, measuring our worth against others becomes a widespread force, shaping our perceptions and influencing our actions. Let us now explore the impact of these comparisons, particularly during the formative years of childhood, as they weave through the fabric of our lives.

Comparisons during childhood

Comparing myself with others has been an all-too-familiar ritual from the earliest threads of my childhood memories. Woven into the societal fabric, it emerged within family circles, resonated throughout the neighborhood, and found its place in the hallowed halls of our school through the voices of our teachers. We were constantly measured against our peers.

Consider the family gatherings during my childhood. A striking scenario would unfold as children huddled around the dinner table. If eight of ten children had devoured every morsel from their plates while two had left their meals partially untouched, they would inevitably become the target of ridicule. The adults would quip, "Look at those children; they have finished everything on their plates, but you have left your plate half-full. Come on, be a good boy, and clear your plate." Unbeknownst to these well-meaning elders, the children may have been satiated or not wanted to eat further. The standard was clear to them: everything on the plate must be consumed.

This culture of comparison extended to our school lives as well. The naughty kids were contrasted with the diligent, perpetually favored students, who always enjoyed the teachers' good graces. The studious individuals who consistently scored well in their exams were held up as exemplars for the rest of us. "Look at them," the teachers would say. "They work diligently and pay unwavering attention in class. You should emulate their commitment, and then, perhaps, you too will earn better grades."

As the children's grades were pitted against each other, an early sense of competition was ingrained. The child who excelled felt the glow of validation, while others struggled with the perceived inadequacy.

The weight of comparison also bore down at home regarding academics. My parents often told me tales of my classmates outshining me academically or boasting about children in our neighborhood who consistently outperformed me. "Look at those children," they would say. "They put in the effort and pay close attention in class and see the grades they have earned." This constant barrage of comparisons shaped my childhood.

Comparisons during adulthood

As we grow older, the comparisons refuse to relent. They persist, often creeping into nearly every facet of our lives. At times, we find ourselves at the receiving end, and at others, we become the instigators, drawing parallels between individuals or pitting one against the other.

These examples demonstrate that comparisons have become deeply ingrained in our society. Mysteriously, they spread through our lives and, at times, unknowingly, draw us into their churning depths. The advent of social media has worsened this phenomenon. People flaunt their extravagant lives, sharing tales of gourmet cuisines, luxurious vacations, and more. Coupled with the pervasive consumer culture, individuals now draw comparisons regarding physical appearances, material possessions, and lavish lifestyles.

It is essential to recognize that comparisons tend to highlight only the glittering facade while concealing the hidden aspects. An illusion is created, fostering the belief that those we compare ourselves to are flawless. It is as if we gaze upon a lush, green meadow on the other side yet fail to see the weeds and thorns hidden from view. This persistent urge to compare ourselves to others contributes to lower self-esteem and anxiety and erects obstacles in our life's journey.

Comparisons leading to poor money spending habits.

In the previous chapter, I shared some poor money-spending habits. One habit not previously mentioned is the tendency to live beyond one's means. The roots of this poor habit are formed mainly due to comparison. As people try to keep up with the standards of others within their society, they tend to go overboard with their spending.

I once witnessed the destructive impact of this constant comparison on a colleague's life. Influenced by a neighbor's cosmetic surgery, his wife yearned for a similar procedure. My colleague vehemently opposed the idea, as the expense of the surgery was beyond his capacity. His fighting the idea led to prolonged conflicts that strained their relationship, ultimately affecting his work performance. After months of debates, he reluctantly agreed, prioritizing the relationship over his reservations. Unfortunately, he had to take a loan for it. His only saving grace was that this loan was taken from our company. The management had agreed to an interest-free loan.

Furthermore, societal norms set lofty standards for significant life events like weddings. People from the same cultural backgrounds are expected to adhere to specific customs and rituals, even if the financial burden is impossible for some.

I distinctly remember a subordinate who faced enormous challenges in his quest to marry. Early in his career, he expressed his intention to get married during a discussion about our annual vacation schedule. However, he remained unsure of the timing due to financial constraints that prevented him from affording the extravagant celebrations that had become customary in his society. Consequently, he postponed his wedding for almost two years, eventually taking a small loan to meet societal expectations.

“

"We buy things we don't need with money we don't have to impress people we don't like."

— **Dave Ramsey.**

”

The Roots of Limiting Beliefs

"I am not good enough."

"I am an idiot."

"I am not good with money."

These are some of the most common limiting beliefs among people. If we take a closer look at how they develop, we can find the roots shaping due to comparisons from childhood to adulthood.

The constant barrage of comparisons with other children during childhood makes a child feel that they may not be good enough. A pivotal moment where a child is faced with embarrassment due to any inadequacy gets ingrained in the subconscious mind, eventually leading to the birth of the limiting belief that they are not good enough.

Similarly, a limiting belief around these points develops when people's intelligence and money status are constantly compared.

The limiting beliefs become a powerful inner voice that usually hinders professional and personal development.

In conclusion, it becomes abundantly clear that comparisons, woven into the fabric of our existence from childhood through adulthood, profoundly influence our lives. As we reflect on the vivid examples from family dinners to societal expectations, it is evident that these comparisons are not mere fleeting observations but persistent companions on our life's journey.

The adverse effects of comparisons resonate deeply, infiltrating our financial habits, influencing major life decisions, and, most dangerously, planting the seeds of limiting beliefs. The glittering facade presented by comparisons often obscures the hidden thorns beneath, fostering feelings of inadequacy and anxiety and erecting formidable obstacles in our pursuit of self-development.

As we navigate through this maze of comparisons, it becomes vitally important to recognize their extensive impact. The following chapters will look into strategies to break free from this cycle, nurturing a path toward self-acceptance and genuine personal growth.

But before we progress to the next chapter, I encourage you to do the below exercise.

Exercise

Self-Reflection:

Set aside a moment of solitude for self-reflection and ask yourself, Which areas of my life do I frequently compare to others? Note these down.

Identifying adverse effects on you:

Reflect on the emotional toll these comparisons take on you. Do they contribute to feelings of inadequacy, anxiety, or low self-esteem?

Question yourself:

Dig deep into the motivations behind your comparisons. Are they driven by societal expectations, personal insecurities, or a desire for external validation?

Chapter 4

Envision Your Fulfilling Life

> *"It is a terrible thing to see and have no vision."*
>
> **- *Helen Keller.***

In the tumultuous currents of life, where uncertainties abound, envisioning your path is like navigating through a garden of choices. Like a gardener's plan, the concept of vision adds structure to the wilderness of existence, guiding us toward a purposeful and fulfilling life.

Introduction to Vision

Vision is the picture of the future that you want to see.

Many individuals drift along in the vast ocean of existence, swept by the currents of circumstances without a distinct destination. They struggle, not because life is inherently harsh, but because they have not taken the time to structure their journey. In the fast-paced world, they speed up their journey without knowing exactly where they are going. It is within this chaos that the profound significance of having a vision for one's life comes to light.

Imagine life as a sprawling garden, nurtured by the seeds of our choices, experiences, and aspirations. Without a guiding vision, this garden risks becoming a haphazard collection of blooms, lacking unity and purpose. A vision serves as the gardener's plan, the master design that brings order to the wilderness and gives our lives direction.

Childhood Vision

What do you want to become?

This was a question frequently asked of children by older people in society. It prompted varied responses. Some children would have no clue about the answer and would reply, "I don't know." Some would hesitate before replying Engineer or Lawyer, the answer coming under the influence of people in their surroundings. The confident children would declare, "Doctor!"

As these children grow up, those who confidently reply might go and become what they desire to become, while some others would have changed their route somewhere along their journey. The child who goes on to become what he desires to become is guided by the vision he may have had, in addition to the environment in which he grew up. Perhaps the child who became a doctor would have several family members as doctors who kept him encouraged and focused on the vision.

Since childhood, we generally tend to have a vision mainly derived from societal expectations. The standard narrative often prescribes obtaining a good degree, securing a stable job, getting married, and settling down. Later, it is about buying a house, children's education, and their marriages. Following these norms might lead to chaos in our lives, and that is why we need to have a master plan to navigate through life's journey.

This vision, however, is not a vague daydream or a fleeting desire. It's a meticulously crafted framework that extends throughout our existence.

Start with envisioning yourself at 80, reflecting on a life well-lived. What do you see? What experiences have shaped you, and what achievements are testaments to your journey?

To be effective, a vision must be broken down into tangible, actionable components — the stepping stones that bridge the present to that envisioned future. These components manifest as long-term and short-term goals. The long-term goals represent the milestones on your journey, while the short-term goals are the practical, achievable steps that push you forward.

In the grand narrative of life, if it were a novel, the vision is the overarching plot, the long-term goals are the central chapters, and the short-term goals are the paragraphs building the narrative. Each paragraph contributes to the overall story, moving steadily towards its climax.

Crafting a vision assumes a lifespan extending to the age of 80. This is not some horrible exercise but a pragmatic one. By considering the entirety of one's existence, we gain a holistic perspective that transcends the immediate challenges of the present. It prompts us to think beyond the superficial and consider the legacy we wish to leave behind.

Roles and responsibilities

Understanding one's role is a prerequisite to crafting a vision. We play different roles in our lives. Some of these roles are mandatory based on our beliefs and principles. These roles include Father, Mother, Son, Daughter, etc. The elective roles are chosen by an individual, for example, an employee at a company or a volunteer in a not-for-profit organization.

You might be wondering why this is a prerequisite. As I mentioned earlier, when I lived on autopilot mode, I always felt guilty about not spending enough time with my family. I also was unable to devote enough time to my self-care. Therefore, to avoid such circumstances, an individual must consider all their roles and the various areas of their life.

Once the roles are identified, each role must be set a minimum level of performance. The performance should be evaluated to understand if any roles have a below-level performance. An excellent performance in one role should not be attained at the cost of poor performance in another.

As an example, usually what happens is a person is excelling at work, getting higher pay and promotions, but on the other hand, doesn't spend quality time with family, which hurts the relationships. Another example is people spending too much time excelling at some volunteer work but not giving enough time to family or self-care.

Have you heard the proverb, "A chain is as strong as its weakest link." It implies that even if some links are strong, if the weakest link breaks, the chain stands to be broken. Similarly, if the performance in a particular role goes below the minimum accepted level, it will hurt other areas of an individual's life, leading to chaos.

Crafting Vision with a framework

As an individual starts crafting their vision, it should include sub-visions for every role played. Each sub-vision contributes to the big vision, ensuring holistic growth and fulfillment. A basic framework also provides a clear path to achieving desired results.

Consider three friends - Jack, Jerry, and John, all aspiring to live a healthy lifestyle. They are asked individually how they plan to live a healthy lifestyle. Jack replies by avoiding junk food. Jerry's answer is I will maintain my weight between 75 to 80 kg, eat healthy food, and walk in the park regularly.

John says he will maintain his weight at 75kg, BMI at 22, Body Fat at 15%, exercise 6 days a week, and eat a healthy diet.

If we look at the response of each one of them, do you notice how elaborate John's reply is and how vague Jack's reply is? What do you think are the chances of Jack's success? I can say from my experience there is very little chance that Jack will succeed in attaining his vision.

As I had mentioned earlier, when the doctor wanted me to start taking medicines to control my blood pressure, I had initially resisted. I had agreed to live a healthy lifestyle. What a healthy lifestyle looked like for me was avoiding junk food and going for walks in the park. As you know by now, I failed in my attempt and eventually had to start taking the medicines.

After a few years, when I needed to change my lifestyle, my vision of a healthy lifestyle looked like I had to eat healthy food, ensure my cholesterol levels were well-balanced, and keep walking regularly.

In pursuit of reversing my medical condition and living a healthy lifestyle, my vision is akin to crafting a finely detailed blueprint for my well-being. Presently, I weigh 73 kgs, and my goal is to reach an optimal 70 kgs. My BMI currently stands at 22.50, and I aim to fine-tune it further to 21.5. The body fat percentage, currently at 22%, is on my radar to be reduced to a lean 16%.

In nutrition, my daily intake revolves around a meticulously balanced diet. I target 1500 to 1600 calories daily, focusing on specific macronutrients. Protein intake is set at 80 grams, carbohydrates at 200 grams, fiber at 30 grams, and fat at 54 grams. This nuanced approach ensures caloric moderation and a focus on the essential components for sustained energy and health.

Ensuring a rejuvenating sleep of at least 6 hours daily is non-negotiable. It is the cornerstone of my holistic well-being strategy. Complementing this, a disciplined workout routine is a commitment I have undertaken six days a week. This regimen encompasses various forms of exercise to cater to multiple aspects of physical fitness.

This detailed vision is a set of aspirations and a roadmap that charts my course toward optimal health. It has evolved from broad lifestyle changes to granular, quantifiable objectives. This approach ensures that each step I take is purposeful, contributing not only to my immediate well-being but also to the sustainable, long-term health I aspire to maintain.

As I navigate this journey, the vision serves as my compass, guiding me through the choices, challenges, and triumphs. It is not just about numbers on a scale or dietary restrictions; it's about cultivating a lifestyle that resonates with vitality, balance, and enduring health.

Delving deeper into my health vision, I have realized that the higher the clarity of one's vision in a particular area of life, the greater the chances of success. Take, for instance, my envisioning of myself as a healthy individual free from dependency on medications. This vision gained strength from a framework of clear, measurable outcomes.

Similarly, every vision must have a path illuminated by measurable outcomes. These outcomes act as milestones, guiding our journey and allowing for tangible progress assessments. As I fine-tune my health vision, I am steadfast in setting precise goals, ensuring that every aspect of my well-being is measurable and attainable.

Why is it important to have a vision?

A vision provides a distinct direction, preventing us from aimlessly drifting with the tide. Like setting the course for a journey, an unclouded vision maps out the path we need to tread. Without this guiding light, we risk being carried away by the currents of circumstance.

Beyond mere direction, a vision is a potent motivator. Picture embarking on a road trip with your family, where reaching your destination demands a 15-hour drive. Along the way, a friend accompanies you, his destination only requiring a 4-hour drive. As you begin the journey, a consensus is reached to pause at your friend's place for a brief break. Once you arrive at your friend's destination, he, exhausted from the trip, refreshes, eats, and retires for a nap. If your wife suggests you do the same, the likelihood of agreeing is slim. With a distinct destination ahead, you're more inclined to resume the journey after the short break.

Moreover, a vision bestows upon us the strength to face challenges head-on. When adversity strikes, the resilience derived from having a grand vision enables us to endure without succumbing to complaints. The enormity of our vision becomes a wellspring of fortitude, propelling us forward with unwavering determination, even in the face of obstacles.

Similarly, in the journey of life, a clear destination acts as a source of motivation. It propels us forward, even in the face of challenges and fatigue. When our goals are vividly defined, we are inspired to persist until we reach our intended destination. The very essence of having a vision lies in the continuous momentum it provides, ensuring that we stay committed to the path we have set for ourselves.

In essence, a vision is more than a distant goal; it is the driving force that propels us beyond the mundane, guiding us through the complexities of life with purpose and determination. The ability to envision our destination not only grants us direction but also fuels the endurance needed to traverse the journey, transforming aspirations into tangible achievements.

“A vision is not just a picture of what could be; it is an appeal to our better selves, a call to become something more.”

— **Rosabeth Moss Kanter.**

The consequence of no clear vision

If we do not have a clear vision, we stand on the brink of unintentionally following an undesired path — often becoming unconscious contributors to someone else's vision. Consider the pervasive influence of advertisements promoting unhealthy food products. These adverts bombard us at supermarkets, on street billboards, and with celebrities endorsing these items. The glossy allure and enticing discounts easily sway us, leading us to consume products that not only jeopardize our health but also inflate the profits of these corporations. Unknowingly, we become integral to a vision that prioritizes profit over our well-being.

This unconscious adherence to a vision extends beyond our dietary choices. It seeps into our healthcare decisions. When we lack a clear vision for our health, we might find ourselves at the mercy of pharmaceutical companies. Consuming products endorsed by flashy marketing campaigns, we unconsciously contribute to the soaring profits of the big pharma industry, especially when we are forced to take medications due to the consequences of unhealthy lifestyle choices.

The absence of a personal vision makes us vulnerable to societal narratives and external influences. We become mere passengers on someone else's journey, inadvertently supporting visions that may not align with our well-being. Our health, choices, and aspirations become entangled in the web of external visions, eroding our autonomy and steering us away from the path that could lead to our true fulfillment.

In essence, without a clear vision, we risk surrendering the reins of our lives to the visions imposed upon us by external forces, be it corporate agendas or societal expectations. Only through the deliberate crafting of our visions can we reclaim power over our destinies and navigate the journey of life with purpose and authenticity.

Historical Examples

History has borne witness to individuals who harbored mammoth visions and, against all odds, manifested those lofty aspirations. Mahatma Gandhi envisioned India breaking free from the shackles of British rule. Martin Luther King dreamt of a future where equal rights prevailed for black people. Nelson Mandela, despite enduring 27 years of imprisonment, six of which were spent in solitary confinement, held steadfast to his vision of a South Africa liberated from apartheid.

These were noble visions anchored in significant causes that transcended personal ambitions. To ascend to such heights, we must first envision ourselves reaching our peak potential in life. As we triumph in our journeys, we gain the capacity to expand our visions, intertwining them with noble causes that can create a massive positive impact in the lives of many.

Even amid immense challenges, Nelson Mandela exemplifies the resilience born from a grand vision. His enduring commitment to a liberated South Africa, forged during years of imprisonment, underscores the transformative power of a vision that extends beyond oneself.

In the wise words of Mahatma Gandhi, "You must be the change you want to see in the world." This underscores the importance of personal transformation aligned with a grand vision. Our aspirations become catalysts for broader societal change when guided by a profound vision.

To wield the transformative power of vision, we must not only dream but also act. Each step in our journey, each achievement, becomes a testament to our potential. As we evolve, so too can our visions, catalyzing positive change in our lives and the world around us.

In essence, the narratives of Gandhi, King, and Mandela underscore that grand visions, fueled by unwavering commitment, can reshape the course of history. They call us to embrace our grand visions, envision a life of peak potential, and, in doing so, become architects of positive change.

As we draw the curtain on this exploration of personal vision, let's transition theory into practice with a transformative exercise.

Exercise

Envision Your Future:

Take a moment to close your eyes and project yourself into the future—imagine your life at 80. Delve into the various areas of your life - your health, wealth, relationships, and beyond. How do you envision these areas unfolding? What achievements and milestones mark your fulfilling journey? Write all the details.

Create Your Network Map:

With this vision in mind, list the names of individuals within your existing network who embody purpose, clarity, and intentional living. Identify those whose experiences and insights could serve as guiding lights on your journey.

Reach Out:

Once your network map is drawn, take the courageous step of reaching out to these individuals. Share your aspirations, seek their wisdom, and learn from their journeys. Human connections are potent catalysts for personal growth.

Seek Professional Guidance:

If, in your network exploration, you find an absence of guiding lights, fear not. The world is abundant with professionals ready to mentor and coach. Invest in your personal growth by seeking out mentors or coaches who align with your vision. Be prepared to invest not just time but also resources in your journey.

Remember the profound words of Mahatma Gandhi, "You must be the change you want to see in the world." Your grand vision is not merely a concept but a dynamic force waiting to be unleashed.

This exercise is not just a task but a commitment to your evolution. By taking these practical steps, you are not only shaping your vision but also forging connections that can illuminate the path to your aspirations.

May your envisioning be vivid, connections meaningful, and your journey toward fulfillment boundless.

If you want me to help you in your journey, kindly click on the link below and fill out the form, and I will get back to you as soon as possible.

https://forms.gle/UyFM1FLjjwZAZwgi6

Chapter 5

Commitment is the Key

> *"You don't know what your abilities are until you make a full commitment to developing them."*
>
> **– *Carol S. Dweck.***

Commitment is an essential cornerstone for success in the grand scheme of transforming visions into reality. It is the structural beam that supports aspirations, the unyielding foundation that turns dreams into tangible achievements.

"I want to achieve financial freedom."

"I want to live a healthy lifestyle."

"I want to make a difference in the world."

These are some common words we hear from people in our daily lives. For most people, these wants remain as they are. Do you know why? The simple reason is that there is a difference between wanting to do something and being committed to it.

Commitment to a cause

Have you heard of Ritesh Agarwal? He founded OYO, the world's most affordable hotel chain. His journey started when he dropped out of college to pursue his entrepreneurial dreams. He had a vision of creating a solution for people looking for affordable hotels around the globe.

He was passionate about travel and observed a gap in the affordable accommodation sector in India. In 2012, at 19, he launched his first venture, Oravel Stays.

Oravel Stays initially began as a platform that allowed travelers to book budget accommodations, including bed and breakfasts, guesthouses, and budget hotels. However, the concept faced difficulties gaining traction, as the market was not ready for such a model then.

Although he did not achieve much success with Oravel Stays, he was committed to the cause of providing affordable accommodation for travelers. He took the initial struggles and limited success of Oravel Stays as a learning experience.

During this challenging period, Ritesh Agarwal personally experienced the difficulties associated with budget accommodations, staying in various small hotels and guesthouses to understand the pain points of both travelers and hotel owners. These experiences fueled his commitment to creating a solution to improve budget accommodations' quality and reliability. He realized that a significant pivot was necessary to address the specific needs of budget travelers.

Ritesh Agarwal demonstrated flexibility and adaptability by pivoting from the original concept of Oravel Stays to the more focused and streamlined model of OYO Rooms. The shift involved standardizing budget hotels to provide a consistent and reliable guest experience. This change in direction from the original concept was a critical decision that played a significant role in OYO's subsequent success.

Despite the initial setbacks, he remained resilient and was determined to achieve his vision of making affordable accommodations accessible to travelers. His passion for the travel industry and belief in the potential for disruption kept him committed to overcoming challenges.

In essence, Ritesh Agarwal's commitment to his cause was fueled by a combination of resilience, adaptability, a deep understanding of the market, and a willingness to learn from failures. His ability to stay focused on the broader vision of providing affordable and standardized accommodations, even in the face of initial challenges, played a pivotal role in OYO's eventual success.

Commitment to self-care and self-love

Let me share the story of Alifiya Lakdawala, my friend and fellow toastmaster. She is a physiotherapist and has been working for more than 20 years.

"Get Up, come on, I know you can do it, I am with you, don't hesitate, here you go."

Her job as a physiotherapist entailed her encouraging the patients to get up, stand up, and move on. She felt blessed to have the ability and skill to give a gentle helping hand to the patients.

In 2003, she got married and had to move in with her husband and mother-in-law. As she adjusted to her new environment, she discovered that she was expecting a child, and within a year of her marriage, she delivered a baby boy.

As a new mother, she was given more privileges. No work, no cooking, mostly eating and sleeping. She could easily finish two portions of an English breakfast and yet be hungry. Within a few months after delivering her first child, she transformed from a slim lady weighing 50 kg to a big fat lady of 92 kg. She was diagnosed with crackling joints, excessive hair fall, and diabetes.

Unfortunately, no one cared about her condition as long as she cared for her loved ones and attended to their needs.

One evening, as she was munching on a pack of Pringles Chips lying in her bed, her son woke up from his slumber. She realized she could not get up as she tried to get up from her bed to attend to her baby. There was no one around to give her a helping hand.

"What have I done to myself?"

"I cannot lift my own body weight."

She had a conversation with herself, feeling deeply emotional. Thinking about how most people, under the illusion of being busy, neglect and abuse their health and their life in general. She realized that she was one of those who had neglected herself.

It was time for her to take care of and love herself, for her to get up and bring a change in her life. In these moments of profound, painful realizations, she committed to herself that she would not neglect herself anymore and would do whatever it took to get back in shape and become a healthy person.

The next day, with full enthusiasm, she was in the park. She could barely walk for a few minutes and had to retire due to the condition she was in.

"OMG!!! I can't do it. This is not for me." She thought to herself.

But then she remembered the gentle hand she gave her patients: "OH, common Alifiya, You can do it, I am with you, you can do it. Do not hesitate, just Get up."

She encouraged herself as she remembered the commitment she had made to herself.

Four years later, her hair fall and diabetes were reversible. She was healthy, strong, and pregnant again.

"Am I going to go through the entire saga of eating and sleeping again?" She asked herself.

"No." was the immediate reply to herself. Never think of going back to your previous version.

As Alifiya shares her story, she says that challenges keep coming, but she always remembers her commitment to herself. Every morning, she wakes up at 4.30 AM to face the challenge the day has in store for her. She says when it is dark, and everybody is asleep, the easiest thing to do is hit the snooze button and return to her warm bed. But her commitment to herself keeps her focused on the tasks ahead.

“

“The quality of a person’s life is in direct proportion to their commitment to excellence, regardless of their chosen field of endeavor.”

— Vince Lombardi.

”

Understanding why we struggle to commit

It is mind-boggling to know that a person desires something but is unwilling to put effort into it. Isn't this the reality? It is simple and logical that one needs to put in some effort to get something. If one cannot commit to something, in reality, what they are saying is I am not willing to put an effort.

That takes us to the question of where this desire has come from. Most likely, it has come from some external source. Commitment is often driven by intrinsic motivation, which comes from within—the desire to achieve something that has originated from their heart rather than some external source.

In the case of Alifiya, it was the realization that if she did not take care of herself, she could end up unable to take care of her family, and in the worst case, she could have to depend on others to manage her activities.

Sometimes, despite having a desire that is not externally influenced, people struggle to commit. In such cases, the endeavor is often a large one. It overwhelms the person, and gradually, they give up. In such cases, one needs to start small by taking micro-actions. For example, if one's lifestyle is sedentary and wants to start walking daily, one can start with the smallest act of wearing a convenient outfit and stepping out of the house on the first day. The next day, add a small activity by walking 50 meters. Every day, keep increasing the distance till you reach the distance that would be a daily standard. As life happens, there might be days when that standard cannot be met; on that day, do the bare minimum.

The reality is that we all have a few minutes to do small activities daily. So, on a day when some unpredictable thing happens, doing the minimum possible helps. Avoiding an activity by saying you will do it tomorrow should not be acceptable; instead, replace it with a shorter activity.

In my case, at the start of my medical condition, when the doctor told me about changing my lifestyle to avoid medicines, the desire to bring that change was internal. I could not stay committed to that path because it got overwhelming. Now, I know about the impact of micro-actions, which helps me stay committed to living a healthy lifestyle. On the days I cannot go for a walk at my scheduled time due to an uncontrollable situation, I ensure that I take some time out from the remaining part of the day to walk, even if it is as little as 5 minutes.

Whether it's a personal life or professional life, commitment threads a standard narrative, weaving tales of determination. Though on different paths, Ritesh Agarwal and Alifiya Lakdawala shared a common attribute - an unwavering commitment to their respective causes.

If we look deeper into the topic of commitment, it becomes evident that the journey is not merely about starting but sustaining, not just dreaming but persisting.

Moving forward, we will unravel another characteristic required to navigate life's challenges. It is the growth mindset. Because commitment, while being the key, demands a mindset that withstands the tests of time and tribulation.

As we reflect on the stories of commitment and the challenges that accompany it, we recognize that commitment is a dynamic force that requires continuous nourishment. Starting with small, intentional actions, acknowledging the source of our desires, and learning to adapt when challenges arise are all crucial components of this journey. In the following pages, we will explore the concept of the growth mindset, an ally in the quest for sustained commitment. So, dear reader, let us embrace the idea that commitment not only opens doors but also shapes the path we tread.

Exercise

Go back to all the exercises you have done in the previous chapters and review your answers where you are looking to bring a positive change in your life.

Ask yourself how committed you are to bringing that positive change.

Chapter 6

The Mindset

> *"Once your mindset changes, everything on the outside will change along with it."*
>
> **- *Steve Maraboli.***

In the vast landscape of personal development, the terrain of our minds determines the course of our journey. It's not just about what we do; it's about how we think. In this chapter, we will look into the profound impact of mindset—the lens through which we view the world.

It is said that the mind is a battlefield, and we engage in a silent war of thoughts every day. Every thought we entertain in this silent war can shape the trajectory of our lives. Do we harbor a fixed mindset, limiting ourselves and seeing challenges as insurmountable obstacles? Or do we embrace a growth mindset, viewing challenges as opportunities for growth and learning?

Mindset, the lens through which we interpret the world, is a silent force that guides our attitudes, behaviors, and, eventually, our outcomes. Before we look into workplace examples, let's briefly define a growth mindset. A growth mindset is characterized by the belief that abilities and intelligence can be developed through dedication and hard work. On the other hand, a fixed mindset sees abilities as innate traits, leading to a desire to appear smart and a tendency to avoid challenges.

Signs of Mindset – Unveiling Workplace Realities

To understand the practical implications of mindset, let's step into the sphere of workplaces. Many of us have encountered bosses with varying leadership styles. Consider the traits of these bosses—some might leave a positive impact, while others leave much to be desired. These distinct qualities often align with the type of mindset they operate with.

Leaders having a fixed mindset generally focus only on their own benefit. When a subordinate works on a report and sends it to them, they forward it to higher management and take full credit for the report without acknowledging the hard work of the subordinate.

On the contrary, we come across bosses looking to benefit their whole team. They are interested in the transformation of all their team members. When they share a report prepared by a team member with higher management, they give due credit to the hard work of that team member. These bosses are operating with a growth mindset.

Drawing from my two decades in accounting and finance, I had the privilege of working with leaders who not only influenced my professional growth but also embodied the principles of a growth mindset. They would share their knowledge openly so that their team could benefit. Moreover, when I prepared any report that was later forwarded to higher management after their review, they acknowledged my work and gave it its due credit. I can easily say that these bosses were operating from a growth mindset.

As is the general principle of life, we will not always have everything rosy. Sometimes, we must see the downside and dark spots, too. Similarly, I have had a fair share of working with bosses who seemed to be working from a fixed mindset. It was generally evident that they did not care for the growth of their team members while being entirely focused on their personal benefits. They would never be open to sharing their knowledge.

What I have learned from working with both these types of leaders is that the mindset of the boss has a significant impact on the performance of the whole team. Working with bosses with a growth mindset helps the team to be more productive. The team members are also driven to perform at their best. Working with leaders with a fixed mindset slows the team's performance. Most team members feel demotivated to give their best.

Mindset of the Masses - General perspectives

In our exploration of mindset, we now focus on the broad view of perspectives held by individuals from diverse backgrounds. From the bustling streets to the quiet corners, each person brings their unique mindset to the table, shaped by circumstances, beliefs, and the ever-evolving experiences of life."

As we look into the collective identities, it becomes apparent that mindsets are not confined to the boardrooms or classrooms but echo through the stories of everyday lives. How individuals, irrespective of their journey, perceive challenges, success, and the ever-constant ebb and flow of life is complex. The mindset, a silent instigator of thoughts, emotions, and actions, manifests differently in the hearts and minds of those navigating life's journey.

In our journey through life, we encounter individuals who exhibit many different traits, sometimes blending characteristics of both growth and fixed mindsets. Life's intricacies often lead people to develop coping mechanisms that may not neatly fit into one category or the other.

For instance, individuals with a growth mindset often demonstrate the following traits:

- Taking ownership of their failures and actions: They analyze setbacks, take responsibility, and strive to learn and grow from their mistakes.
- Talking about ideas and the well-being of people: Their conversations revolve around constructive topics, contributing to the betterment of themselves and others.
- Looking for little joys in every situation: They maintain a positive attitude, finding opportunities for growth and happiness even in challenging circumstances.

On the contrary, individuals with a fixed mindset may exhibit the following traits:

- Blaming external factors and circumstances for their failures: They attribute their shortcomings to external forces, avoiding personal responsibility.
- Gossiping and backbiting: Their conversations tend to focus on the shortcomings of others, often engaging in negative discussions.

- Complaining about every little problem: They tend to vocalize dissatisfaction with various aspects of their lives.

When we discuss the above examples, it's crucial to recognize that human traits are diverse and dynamic. People are complex, and the interplay between fixed and growth mindsets is not always straightforward. Our development requires us to be aware of our shortcomings and continuously work on improving them.

A few years back, I had a colleague who would bring snacks to the office and share them with me. Unfortunately, as we sat down to eat, he often started gossiping. Despite my efforts to discourage this behavior, he persisted. Despite his fixed mindset tendencies, this colleague had moments of generosity and camaraderie. Understanding these nuances is essential as we navigate the multifaceted landscape of the human mindset.

Another example is of a close relative. He has a loving and caring nature and always wants the well-being of others. But the problem is that he keeps worrying about little things. He sees problems all around.

I have realized through such experiences that people who see scarcity around them tend to lean towards a fixed mindset, while those who see abundance all around tend to lean towards a growth mindset.

One trait that helps reshape and improve an individual's mindset is the trait of Gratitude. Gratitude has been associated with various positive psychological and emotional outcomes, and intentionally practicing gratitude can contribute to a more optimistic mindset.

Moving forward, let's look into the transformative power of gratitude in shaping one's mindset.

Power of Gratitude

As we have seen, some of the characteristics of individuals with a fixed mindset are focusing on problems, gossiping, and blaming external factors for their failure. But if we look deeply into these people's lives, they would have been blessed with many resources. If they focus on the resources they have in hand, they can easily find solutions to their problems.

Gratitude is just a realization of the resources one has and being thankful for that. Gratitude helps because it cleans the lenses through which you look at the world.

When I look back on my experiences when I lost my job, in the initial days, I was worried about the immediate future. Constant negative thoughts about what would happen kept flooding my mind. During this time, I came across a video of Nouman Ali Khan, an Islamic speaker who spoke about the significance of gratitude. He explained how, many positive things will undoubtedly happen in every challenging situation. You need to focus on these aspects and be thankful for that.

After I heard this lecture, I started to think about the positives in my life. That is when I realized the one thing I constantly complained about was a lack of time. My focus shifted toward how I can utilize my time for my personal growth. I was grateful for the time I had to work on myself and spend quality time with my family.

This is how I was guided by the divine power toward reading personal development books. Focusing on one positive from an adverse situation opened growth paths for me. I got hold of the book The Magic of Thinking Big, which led me to join Toastmasters. I gradually transformed from a shy person who was scared to voice his opinion and speak in public to a confident man delivering speeches.

The practice of gratitude didn't eliminate challenges but empowered me to approach them with a growth mindset. I learned to appreciate the abundance of positive elements in my life, no matter how small. As a result, I became more open to learning, growing, and embracing opportunities.

“

“Gratitude is a powerful process for shifting your energy and bringing more of what you want into your life. Be grateful for what you already have, and you will attract more good things.”

— **Rhonda Byrne.**

”

The Inspirational Story of Sheetal Devi

As we have seen the transformative power of gratitude, let us draw inspiration from real-life stories that embody the strength of the human spirit. One such remarkable tale is that of Sheetal Devi, a 16-year-old archer from Loidhar village in the North Indian State of Jammu and Kashmir.

Sheetal was born on 10th January 2007 with Phocomelia, a rare congenital disorder that causes under-developed limbs. Sheetal was the first and only armless female archer to compete internationally. She won three medals at the Asian Para Games in Hangzhou, including two gold medals from the mixed doubles and women's individual events. Sheetal started training with the bow-and-arrow just two years ago and has already achieved so much.

Sheetal was fond of climbing trees using her legs. Not having arms didn't deter her from climbing trees. This leisure activity significantly strengthened her upper body, helped improve her athleticism, and made scouts take notice of her talent in archery during a local event organized by the Indian Army in 2021.

Her mentors initially tried to get her a prosthetic arm so that she could train for archery. Unfortunately, this idea could not materialize; thus, they felt it would end Sheetal's hope of competing.

Not losing hope after failing to get a prosthetic arm, Sheetal began training at the Shri Mata Vaishno Devi Shrine Board Sports Complex in Katra. She kept a positive mindset, thinking she would not give up if this did not work out. Instead, she would try harder.

"No one has any shortcomings. One just needs to work a little harder." These are the profound words of Sheetal.

The disorder she has had since birth could easily have been an excuse. However, the traits of taking ownership of her actions and the willingness to put in the hard work showed her growth mindset.

Sheetal Devi's victory is an example of the triumph of the human spirit against all odds. Her story is a testament to the power of mindset.

In closing our exploration of mindset, we have traversed diverse landscapes—from the intricate dynamics of workplaces to the nuanced perspectives of individuals in their everyday lives. We looked into the transformative power of gratitude and witnessed, through Sheetal Devi's inspiring journey, the triumph of a growth mindset against all odds. As you absorb the stories shared, remember this: the mindset you cultivate is the compass guiding your journey. Just as Sheetal shaped her destiny through unwavering determination, each of us possesses the potential to harness the transformative power of mindset.

Reflect on the silent battles within your mind, ponder the wisdom in these pages, and recognize that embracing a growth mindset isn't just a choice; it's a key to unlocking doors to untapped possibilities. Now, as you embark on the transformative journey of breaking free, carry with you the profound realization that your mindset shapes your challenges and victories.

As we wrap up this chapter, take a moment to engage in the following activity. This reflective exercise is designed to guide you through an introspective journey, allowing you to unlock new perspectives and support personal growth.

Exercise

Rate your mindset:

Below is a sample exercise for you to reflect on your mindset. Give yourself ratings in each line such that the total under each line's negative and positive ratings equals 10.

For example, in line 4, if you tend to worry more often but sometimes feel abundant, you can rate worry as 7 or 8 and the corresponding positive comment of abundance as 3 or 2.

After you rate all the lines, total the negative and positive ratings and see where you stand. Let me reiterate that this is just a sample for you to keep reflecting on your mindset daily. There can be many aspects that you need to think of to evaluate your mindset.

Line	Negative	Ratings	Positive	Ratings
1	Gossip about other people.		Talk about the well-being of others and bright ideas.	
2	Blame external factors and circumstances for failures.		Take ownership of my actions and failures.	
3	Complain about every problem.		Look for joy in every situation.	
4	Worry about the future.		Feel content and abundant.	
5	Miser		Generous	

Gratitude Practice:

Develop a daily gratitude practice for the next 21 days. Each day, write down three things you are grateful for. Ensure that you feel thankful within because genuine gratitude is from the heart, not by putting it in words. Reflect on how focusing on gratitude enhances your awareness of the positive aspects of your unique life.

Chapter 7

You Are Unique

> *"Life is the most difficult exam. Many people fail because they try to copy others, not realizing that everyone has a different question paper."*
>
> ***– Dr. APJ Abdul Kalam.***

In the sprawling library of our lives, each person is a book with a story entirely their own. This chapter encourages you to explore the journey of self-discovery, revealing a simple truth we may overlook—the unmatched uniqueness within each person. Imagine walking through the aisles, each book telling a distinct story. Intricately woven into the pages, your story forms a literary masterpiece that stands alone in its richness and depth.

Embracing Our Uniqueness

We are not replicas; each one of us is an original. Our circumstances, personalities, experiences, and beliefs form a kaleidoscope that cannot be replicated in any other individual. The temptation to compare oneself to others is widespread, lurking in the corners of our minds. However, it's crucial to recognize the futility and detriment of such comparisons. Comparing your journey to someone else's is like comparing a painter's brushstrokes to a musician's melody—they belong to different domains.

The story of Rajendra Singh

Rajendra Singh, often called the "Waterman of India," is an environmentalist and water conservationist known for his efforts in water management and revitalizing traditional water harvesting techniques.

In 1985, Rajendra Singh founded the non-governmental organization (NGO) Tarun Bharat Sangh (TBS) to conserve water and promote sustainable development. The organization works towards water management, ecological restoration, and community development.

Rajendra Singh is known for reviving ancient water conservation methods. His efforts have contributed to replenishing groundwater levels and restoring water sources in several drought-prone areas. Much of his work has been concentrated in the arid regions of the Indian State of Rajasthan, where water scarcity is a significant issue. He has transformed barren landscapes into green and fertile areas through community-led initiatives.

Rajendra Singh's contributions to water conservation have earned him numerous awards, including the Ramon Magsaysay Award in 2001 and the Stockholm Water Prize in 2015.

Rajendra Singh's story is unique because of the path he chose. His focus was on grassroots-level water conservation using traditional wisdom at a time when modern techniques often take precedence. His unconventional approach showcases the power of embracing one's unique path.

Just as Rajendra Singh found his unique calling, let's now look into the distinctive journey of Nawazuddin Siddiqui.

The story of Nawazuddin Siddiqui

In the entertainment industry, where glamour often overshadows grit, Nawazuddin Siddiqui emerges as a rare thread weaving a story of unparalleled resilience and raw talent. His journey from the humble lanes of Budhana, a small town in Uttar Pradesh, India, to the dazzling lights of Bollywood is not just a story of success; it's a testament to the transformative power of staying true to oneself in an industry that often demands conformity.

Let's unravel the layers of Nawazuddin Siddiqui's narrative. This story transcends the screen, revealing the extraordinary within the ordinary and proving that sometimes, the most captivating tales are those written with grit, passion, and an unwavering commitment to authenticity.

In a domain where conventional looks and backgrounds often define success, Nawazuddin Siddiqui stood out. His physical appearance and unconventional background were initially met with skepticism and disapproval, echoing the prevalent norms of the industry. However, Nawazuddin's authenticity, commitment to his craft, and refusal to conform to stereotypical expectations became his greatest assets.

Amidst societal expectations to fit into a predetermined mold, Nawazuddin Siddiqui fearlessly embraced his uniqueness. He didn't succumb to the pressure of altering his appearance or diluting his identity to fit into the conventional Bollywood narrative. Instead, he celebrated his individuality, turning what could have been perceived as weaknesses into his strengths.

His journey involved overcoming financial constraints, societal norms, and even rejection within the film industry due to his unconventional looks and lack of a conventional Bollywood hero appearance. Nawazuddin Siddiqui's success, therefore, is not just a story of breaking into an industry but a narrative of redefining industry standards by being unapologetically himself.

In several interviews, Siddiqui has discussed his challenges and how his uniqueness became a distinguishing factor in his roles. His story is not just one of rising against the odds but of using one's distinctiveness as a tool for success.

Despite these obstacles, Nawazuddin Siddiqui pursued his passion for acting, confident that his talent was unique. Over time, he gained recognition for his talent and versatile performances, establishing himself as one of the most acclaimed actors in the Indian film industry.

Nawazuddin Siddiqui's story exemplifies how individuals may encounter resistance and opposition when choosing unconventional career paths, especially in industries perceived as unpredictable or non-traditional. His success underscores the importance of perseverance and staying true to one's passion despite societal pressures and expectations.

The Futility of Comparison

Every person's path is uniquely their own, and comparing your journey to someone else's is like measuring an apple against an orange. The circumstances that shape your story are exclusive to you. Therefore, the only meaningful comparison is with your past self. Evaluate your growth, celebrate your progress, and learn from your experiences. The only competition worth engaging in is the one against your former self.

Influenced by societal norms, we may perceive life as a race, with constant comparisons prevalent in various aspects. People are often measured against their peers, relatives, or classmates. However, it doesn't have to be this way, as everyone's journey is inherently different, shaped by diverse life experiences, perspectives, values, and beliefs.

Everyone should evaluate themselves at periodic intervals. Align your evaluations with your long-term vision and the outcomes you aim to achieve. Regularly assess your growth by comparing yourself with the person you were three months, six months, and one year ago. Reflect on what you have learned during these intervals and your improvements.

If you lack progress, use it as motivation to enhance yourself. However, avoid the trap of comparing yourself to others. Celebrate your progress, and as you look back at your past self, acknowledge the positive changes you've embraced. Personal growth is a journey, and each step forward is a testament to your commitment to becoming the best version of yourself.

Reflecting on my journey, I recognize that until six years ago, I had never read personal development books. This realization might seem awkward, leading me to question why I had not started this exploration earlier.

Always remember that your actual competition is with your past self. Seek the unique path you wish to tread and embark on that journey without being distracted by the routes others are taking.

Just as Rajendra Singh and Nawazuddin Siddiqui remained focused on their distinctive paths—Rajendra utilizing traditional water conservation methods and Nawazuddin undeterred by societal norms in his pursuit of acting—embrace your journey without succumbing to external pressures or comparisons. Your uniqueness is your strength on the path to personal growth.

Making the Most of Your Time

Within the shared dimension of time, everyone is granted the same 24 hours every day. However, the true essence lies not in comparing how others allocate their time but in optimizing your own. These precious hours shape your journey, influenced by the choices you make. Are you dedicating time to personal growth, fostering relationships, and pursuing your passions? Understanding the inherent value of time is crucial, as once it slips away, it cannot be reclaimed.

As I have mentioned several times, my constant complaint was the lack of time. This was because my life lacked a vision; therefore, there was no structure for how I spent my time. However, as I worked on personal development, various methods and practices helped optimize my time. Notably, I learned that there is no one-size-fits-all approach. We must constantly implement and evaluate methods, fill gaps, and refine our strategies.

Initially, I faced difficulties accomplishing tasks, realizing I spent time on non-essential activities and planned unrealistic goals. Recognizing our human nature, I moved away from a mechanical approach, embracing a more flexible perspective.

While training for The Incredible You Coach program, I discovered the power of breaking down long-term outcomes into smaller, achievable parts.

Therefore, every individual needs to prioritize activities and stay disciplined in achieving them. Weekly evaluations are essential to identify time allocation patterns. In the modern age, mindless scrolling through social media consumes valuable time. We can optimize our time by scheduling such activities during low-energy periods or daily commutes.

The most crucial lesson I have learned is to put a value on your time. Calculating the hourly value based on monthly income is effective for working individuals. This practice fosters consciousness of how time is spent. For instance, ordering groceries online may seem costlier, but when we put value on our time, the convenience outweighs the cost.

Every day offers 86,400 seconds. Don't let a brief negative interaction ruin the remaining hours. Forgive, forget, and move forward. To dwell on the past or worry about the future wastes the precious seconds of today.

Our life reflects how we spend our time. So, we must optimize our time by embracing our unique journey.

“

“Time is the most valuable coin in your life. You and you alone will determine how that coin will be spent. Be careful that you do not let other people spend it for you.”

— **Carl Sandburg.**

”

Embracing the Infinite Treasures of God

God's treasures are unlimited and infinite. In a world that sometimes seems bound by limitations, shifting our mindset towards abundance is essential. Abundance is not just a state of wealth; it's a state of mind. When you approach life with a mindset of abundance, you attract opportunities, blessings, and joy. In every step, envision the boundless treasures that await.

Conditioning since childhood leads us to conform to societal standards. When we tread on unchartered territory, we worry about people's opinions. Don't let the fear of criticism hold you back.

Embarking on a unique path may invoke the fear of failure. However, remember that failure is not the opposite of success; it's a stepping stone towards it. Take that leap of faith, for doors of abundance often swing open in uncertainty. Your uniqueness is not a liability but an asset. Embrace the unknown with courage, and you will find that the universe conspires in your favor.

Exercise

Self-Reflection:

Take a few moments to reflect on and write down three aspects of your life that make you unique. Consider your experiences, skills, and values. How have these unique aspects shaped your journey so far?

Evaluate Your Growth:

Create a timeline of your personal growth over the past year. Identify critical milestones, challenges, and achievements. Reflect on how these experiences have contributed to your life.

Comparison Detox:

Challenge yourself to a "comparison detox" for the next week. When you compare your journey to others, pause and redirect your focus to your progress—Journal about the positive changes you observe.

Chapter 8

Patience and Resilience

> *"Many of life's failures are people who did not realize how close they were to success when they gave up."*
>
> **– *Thomas Edison.***

Life has its ups and downs. We all face different challenges in our lives. Some situations are easy to handle, while others can be difficult. Sometimes, we must face towering challenges that appear as daunting as Mount Everest. Such challenges can make or break us. How we deal with it shapes our character and destiny.

If we are patient during such challenging times and show some resilience in overcoming these challenges, we develop character and strength to reach great heights in our lives.

The Story of Arunima Sinha

In the shadow of the world's highest peak, we find stories defying the limits of human endurance. One such tale is that of Arunima Sinha, a beacon of resilience who conquered the summit with a prosthetic leg. Her journey is not just a mountaineering feat but a testament to the indomitable spirit that arises from patience and resilience.

Arunima Sinha's journey is both harrowing and inspiring. Her story began with a tragic incident that changed her life forever.

In 2011, Arunima, a national-level volleyball player in India, traveled by train from Lucknow to Delhi. Unfortunately, she encountered a group of robbers who attempted to snatch her gold chain. Arunima was thrown out of a moving train in her courageous attempt to fend them off. Coincidently, another train was passing by on the adjacent railway track. At first, she banged into the other train before she fell on the tracks. After the trains had passed, she tried to get up only to realize that one of her legs was cut. The fall resulted in severe injuries. The circumstances were dire; she lay by the tracks, injured and in need of immediate medical attention. Although she was screaming for help, nobody rescued her during the night. It took several hours before she received some help. In the morning, some local villagers took her to the hospital.

The gravity of her injuries was staggering. Her legs were severely damaged. The doctors had to amputate one leg to save her life. There was no anesthesia or blood available to proceed with her surgery. As she heard the doctors discussing her case, she told the doctors that she had endured the pain all through the night and she would bear the pain in the absence of anesthesia. After listening to this courageous statement from her, the Doctors and other hospital staff decided to donate one unit of blood each. Eventually, the surgery went ahead, and her leg was amputated.

This marked the beginning of a long and arduous journey towards recovery. Arunima faced physical pain, emotional turmoil, and the daunting challenge of relearning how to navigate the world with a prosthetic limb.

As she lay in her hospital bed recovering from the severe injuries, she got to hear rumors about her. It was said that she was traveling without a ticket, and she threw herself out of the running train to escape official punishment. Another report mentioned that she wanted to commit suicide.

However, rather than succumbing to despair, Arunima found resilience within herself. Her spirit refused to be broken by the circumstances. She didn't just want to recover; she aimed to achieve something extraordinary. From her heart, mind, and soul, she decided she would prove to the world what she was and what she could do. Her dream to climb Mount Everest was born from this fire within her.

The road to Everest was paved with immense challenges. She had to undergo rigorous physical training to prepare for the strenuous climb. She found a mentor in the form of Madam Bachendri Pal, who had climbed Mount Everest in 1984.

Arunima's financial situation was also a hurdle, as funding such an endeavor was an uphill battle. Yet, she embarked on this monumental journey through sheer determination and the support of well-wishers.

"Arunima, with the physical handicap that you have, to think of climbing Mount Everest, you have won a big inner battle. You have mentally already climbed it; now you need to go and do it." Her mentor's words echoed in her ears as she embarked on this journey in 2013.

As she started this journey, the enormity of the task ahead dawned upon her, but she relentlessly persevered. When the local companion, the Sherpa, came to know that she had one prosthetic leg and another one had a rod in it, he declined to accompany her as he felt he would also be risking his life. Arunima and her support team eventually convinced the Sherpa to accompany her.

The journey was filled with several hurdles. She acclimatized to all situations, from treading rocky trails to icy paths. As she moved from one camp to another, Arunima also witnessed several dead bodies. These were the bodies of people who also had the lofty ambitions of climbing Mount Everest but could not make it. Arunima felt goosebumps looking at the dead bodies, but she focused on her journey and said to herself she would complete her mission and come back alive. She had the belief that how one thinks, the body responds accordingly.

On 21st May 2013, Arunima Sinha made history by becoming the first female amputee to climb Mount Everest. Her triumph was not just a personal victory but a symbol of resilience, courage, and the unyielding human spirit.

Her story serves as a ray of hope and a testament to the power of perseverance, inspiring countless individuals worldwide. Arunima didn't let her circumstances define her. Instead, she defined her circumstances through her unwavering willpower, showcasing that even the loftiest summits can be conquered with resilience and patience.

We learn from the story of Arunima Sinha that no matter how big a calamity strikes our lives, we have immense potential to overcome it. It requires us to patiently evaluate the situation and draw a map to navigate the path ahead.

“Our greatest weakness lies in giving up. The most certain way to succeed is always to try just one more time.”

— **Thomas Edison.**

Nurturing Patience on the Journey to Success

Amidst the rush for instant success, we often underestimate the silent force of patience. Like the slow and steady ascent to Everest's peak, outstanding achievements require time. Patience is not passive waiting but a conscious choice to endure, learn, and grow. It is the unwavering belief that every step forward, no matter how small, contributes to the eventual triumph.

When they start working on something big, most people put in a lot of effort. They tend to give up because they cannot see the short-term results. They do not realize that each small step they take has its significance in the long term. As this realization does not dawn upon them, the opportunities slip away, and the hard work goes down the drain. In such times, every individual should trust the power of small, consistent actions because every step to achieve a goal is a small success. The focus should be on the journey rather than the destination. Every step in the journey should be appreciated.

Cricket Match Lesson: Patience and Resilience

Drawing inspiration from the match between Australia and Afghanistan at the 2023 Cricket World Cup, we can see an example of resilience and patience. Chasing a target of 292 runs to win, Australia's score read 91 for the loss of 7 wickets in the 19th over. From that point onwards, what already looked like a mammoth target became more difficult when their last recognized batsman, Glen Maxwell, started cramping up and could not run freely. Despite this situation, Australia's captain, Pat Cummins, played a patient inning and supported Maxwell, who showed resilience in the face of adversity. Maxwell played a historic innings, completing his double-century and taking Australia to victory. They snatched victory from the jaws of defeat by showing Patience and Resilience.

This was only a cricket match, but we can take inspiration from it that when the going gets tough, we must keep moving ahead, pass small milestones, and inch towards the target.

Arunima Sinha's Impact on My Journey

Looking back on those pivotal moments in my life, where the weight of health concerns loomed large and the prospect of a lifetime tethered to medication weighed heavily on my mind, I realized that my initial attempts to steer clear of this path faltered because I did not follow the instructions of the doctor consistently.

After I started the medication, I followed the routine regularly for a few years. Later, after reading and listening to stories of people who successfully reversed their medical condition, I decided to try the same but never took proper guidance on the subject.

I had read about the inspiring story of Arunima Sinha. Still, it never really catalyzed any change in my life until I attended an event on 25th August 2023 in Mumbai where Aruna Sinha spoke and narrated her story live on stage.

Arunima's story, resonating through the halls of that Mumbai event, acted as a catalyst, illuminating the power of resilience with me. Her unwavering strength in the face of tragedy ignited a spark, reminding me that her determination to defy circumstances mirrors my aspirations.

Thus, my journey toward living a holistically healthy lifestyle commenced. With newfound determination, I sought professional guidance, embarking on a path that aimed to manage and conquer my health challenges. Educating myself on this subject has become a cornerstone. I have been ushering in lifestyle changes, particularly in dietary habits. I am also following a physical fitness routine. These changes that I have made are already making a positive impact on my health, and I know that with continued efforts, my medical condition will be reversed.

As I stand poised on this path, I understand the indispensable roles of patience and resilience in transforming aspirations into reality. The stories I have shared are not just anecdotes; they are invitations for you to seize these virtues and weave them into the fabric of your ambitions.

Exercise

Reflect on your life journey and acknowledge the dreams or challenges that have slipped from your grasp because you gave up. Think of all your aspirations and desires that once seemed impossible yet remain close to your heart. Write them down, for in doing so, you renew their significance in your life.

Evaluate their significance now. Are they still of importance to you? If the answer is a resounding "yes," channel your determination into a structured action plan. Craft a roadmap, breaking down the monumental task into smaller, attainable steps.

In your journey towards this ambition, acknowledge the strength in seeking support. Think of those individuals who can be part of your support team. List their names and reach out to them.

As you reach out to these people, be courageous and share your aspirations openly. Engage with this support network and invite them to join you on this voyage.

And so, armed with patience as your compass and resilience as your shield, embark on this expedition. Embrace the mantra of persistence, toiling diligently towards your goal while never yielding to the lure of surrender.

Chapter 9

Yes! You Can Do It!

> *"It is never too late to be who you might have been."*
>
> **– *George Elliot.***

As we travel in our journey of life, there comes a point where the whispers of our inner critic grow louder, drowning the aspirations that once danced freely in the canvas of our imagination. This chapter is an invitation to recognize that relentless voice, the doubter within, and to embark on a journey of silencing it. For within the depths of self-discovery lies the key to unlocking the dormant dreams and rewriting the narrative of our lives.

Recognizing the Inner Critic

As they grow older, most people usually think of how to ensure they are surviving in a fast-paced world. Any ideas of growth are quashed by themselves. Their inner voice discourages them from having big ideas.

Often, an idea pops into our minds, and we reject it instantly. The inner voice tells us that we cannot execute the idea. It tells you that only a special person can execute the idea, and that person is not you.

Have you ever wondered why this happens? It is mainly because of the conditioning since childhood and the perspectives developed through life experiences.

Children at a young age are fearless. Their ideas and imaginations are limitless. Their minds come up with all kinds of possibilities. Unfortunately, as these children grow up, their world places limits and boundaries around their ideas. The existing limiting beliefs of society are passed on to future generations.

As we go through our lives, different experiences shape our perspectives on every situation. Do you wonder how one situation brings different reactions from different people? When the weather forecast predicts heavy rainfall, some people will be happy that they can enjoy the rain by having hot tea with fresh dumplings. On the other hand, some people will get anxious thinking about the gloomy skies and flooded roads. The sales staff at various stores will dread the expected low footfall due to the heavy rains.

These reactions come from past experiences that act as references. People happy to know that it will rain would have had an earlier experience of having tea and dumplings while enjoying the rainfall. The person getting anxious about flooded roads would have had an experience of being stuck.

We must realize all these are just situations that happened in the past that were not under our control. We cannot keep imagining a situation's negatives and repeating them in our minds.

If we keep imagining and thinking that life is difficult, we will feel the pain of a difficult life and make ourselves miserable. On the contrary, if we imagine life is beautiful, we will see the beauty of life even in challenging times. This will help us to overcome the obstacles that come our way.

Impact of a book

In my transformation, after implementing the teachings from the book The Magic of Thinking Big, I witnessed a gradual shift in me. I always tried to sit in the front rows when attending events or workshops. I joined Toastmasters and was delivering speeches with ease. Standing in front of a crowd and speaking was something I dreaded most of my life, but now I enjoy it.

When I reflected upon the impact of this book on my life, I thought it was such a wonderful feeling to see the result. A book written in the 1950s, the author died in the 1980s, but his teachings were still alive long after his death. That is when an idea popped up into my mind. I thought to myself, I should do something similar. I told myself I would write a book that would impact people's lives even after my death. Unfortunately, the inner voice killed my thoughts at that exact moment. How will you write a book? You cannot even draft a simple email to your boss. You cannot write a proper official letter when corresponding with different authorities. These were pieces of evidence my inner voice gave me as it discouraged me from thinking about becoming an author.

The idea of writing a book used to pop into my mind occasionally, only for me to reject it instantly as my inner voice shouted out, no! You cannot do it.

Today, as you read this book, I want you to realize that what once seemed impossible for me has become a reality. The idea

I repeatedly dismissed due to my inner critic has been executed despite the limiting beliefs.

So, what changed? How did I silence my inner voice? How did I overcome my limiting beliefs?

Just as my inner voice discouraged me from thinking about becoming an author, it also prevented me from many other things. I am sure many of you can relate to this.

Seeking Guidance

The turning point in my life came through introspection. I struggled in different areas of my life and wanted to bring a positive change. Thankfully, in this Internet age, we have instant access to a vast reservoir of information. I realized I needed to get the help of a life coach to navigate the challenges of my life.

After various research, I shortlisted a couple of coaches and eventually took the services of a Life Coach who ticked all the boxes. I engaged with him over nine months in 2021, discussing my life challenges. During these sessions, he asked some profound questions that made me look within myself and helped me find answers that would be the guiding light on my path of self-development.

Before the life coaching sessions, I thought of changing my professional career. I wanted to do some meaningful work. But whenever I thought about a career change, my inner voice would tell me that I am a Commerce graduate with an accounting background. I only had the experience of working as an Accounting and Finance Professional.

What can you do now when you are already in your forties? This was one of the self-doubting questions being asked to me by my inner voice.

Through the conversations I had with my coach, I decided that I would become a Life Coach. As we discussed the path towards becoming a life coach, we concluded that joining a community of coaches would be best.

Before these sessions with my coach, I was flowing with the tide of life, not knowing where I was heading. My sessions with my coach helped me decide on a direction in my life journey. Can you imagine a driver driving a Public Transport Bus and not knowing the bus's route? It is improbable, yet I felt as if I was the bus driver of my life who did not know the bus route I was driving.

With the help of my coach, I drew a roadmap of where I wanted to go in life over the next ten years. However, the immediate plan was to join a coaching community in the next 12 to 24 months. This would give me the training required to qualify as a Life Coach and help me do more meaningful work.

I joined world-renowned coach Arfeen Khan's "The Incredible You Coach Training Academy." As I started my coach training, I immersed myself in human personality's intricacies. I began to implement the learnings from the training sessions. The thoughts of becoming an author seeped into my mind more often, and as I discussed it with my coach, I was encouraged to pursue it simultaneously with my coaching training.

I shared my past experiences with my coach. I confided in him about my persistent self-doubt regarding writing a book.

He posed a question that would alter my perspective forever: "Farhan, why does your inner voice discourage you?"

I hesitated before responding, "Drafting an email to my boss or writing any official letter has always been a struggle. Writing a book feels monumental compared to those tasks."

My coach, empathizing with me, offered a profound insight, "Negative thoughts are inevitable. What we must learn is how to transform them into positive ones."

"But how?" I asked.

"Recall an achievement you believed impossible," he suggested.

"I never thought I could speak in public, but I have delivered numerous speeches at various events," I admitted.

"How did you achieve this success?" he asked, to which I replied by joining Toastmasters and learning to deliver speeches.

He smiled and said, " Now you have evidence that when you tried something new and put in the required effort, you succeeded in what seemed impossible. Let this triumph silence your inner voice whenever a novel idea comes to your mind.

This conversation with my coach spurred me to move forward in my quest to write a book and become an author.

Just like this conversation helped me, I urge you to help yourself whenever your inner voice discourages you by making this conversation a reference point for you.

Always remember that our brain looks for some evidence to give us the green light to go ahead and pursue a new goal. Overcoming the fear of public speaking by joining Toastmasters and delivering speeches was the evidence I gave to my brain when I followed the goal of writing this book.

Reflections on my journey

Looking back at my life, I can easily distinguish between the person I was before 2018 and the person I was after 2018.

The person that I was before 2018 was a man who was stagnant and settled in living a life way below my potential. I was navigating the tides of life without a compass. My days felt like an endless loop, having a familiar uninspiring routine. Imagine a vast, stagnant pond, its surface reflecting a clouded sky. I moved through each day without a clear sense of purpose, my potential submerged beneath the still waters, dormant and untouched.

After 2018, I am constantly looking to grow as a person. I have emerged from the cocoon of complacency, my wings unfurling to reveal a spectrum of possibilities. The once-stagnant pond has transformed into a flowing river, carving new paths and irrigating the previously dry land of my aspirations.

Thinking about my life experiences takes me to the famous quote of Benjamin Franklin: Some people die at 25 and are not buried until 75. I understand from this quote that some people, despite being physically alive, lose their zest for life at a young age and accept the status quo, which causes their true potential to remain untapped.

As I continued my journey of self-discovery, I uncovered the subtle ways in which negative thoughts can embed themselves in the subconscious mind, like seeds taking root in fertile soil. Often planted by external influences or past experiences, these thoughts can sprout into constant worry and stagnation if left unaddressed.

The subconscious mind, like a data bank, stores beliefs and impressions formed over time. Negative experiences, criticisms, or self-doubts can seep into this data bank, influencing our perceptions and actions. It's a silent process, often unnoticed, yet it plays a significant role in shaping our mindset.

Constant worry becomes the echo of these negative seeds, a persistent hum in the background of our thoughts. It's the subtle undercurrent that whispers, "You can't," "You're not enough," or "What if you fail?" This worry, if unchecked, can anchor us in a state of perpetual stagnation.

But the good news is that just as negative thoughts can take root, so can positive ones. The mind needs to be planted with seeds of positivity and optimism.

I encountered individuals who, despite facing their share of negative seeds, managed to break through the soil and reach for the sunlight of growth. Their stories serve as a guiding light, illuminating the path toward personal development and fulfillment.

As we explore the transformative power of overcoming self-doubt, let's look into another inspiring journey. Vikram Joshi's story beautifully illustrates the power of challenging our inner critic.

Vikram Joshi is my friend and a fellow Toastmaster who joined Toastmasters before me. For almost five years, he was sleepwalking in his journey of Toastmasters. He never regularly attended the meetings. He delivered speeches and actively participated in the meetings on rare occasions. Last year, when I was elected president of my club, I asked him to nominate himself as vice president of education. Initially, he obliged, but after the elections, he stepped down, saying he could not do justice to the role.

Fast forward to the present day, he is currently the President of our club, and simultaneously, he is also the Area Director under which our club falls. He wears multiple hats during our meetings, taking additional responsibilities and completing them as best as possible.

"Unless you don't dive in the swimming pool, you will not learn swimming," says Vikram, sharing his leadership experiences to inspire others.

In the past, his mind was tangled in the loop of negative thoughts. He used to worry about him not being good enough. With the help and encouragement of several mentors, a belief was instilled in him that he has the potential to excel in various roles.

“

“Twenty years from now, you will be more disappointed by the things you didn’t do than by the ones you did. So, throw off the bowlines. Sail away from the safe harbor. Catch the trade winds in your sails. Explore. Dream. Discover.”

— **Mark Twain.**

”

Overcoming Negative Thoughts

Just as Vikram and I have overcome the negative thoughts to come out of mediocrity, so can you. The first step is to become aware of negative thoughts as they arise. Observe the thoughts without judgment. Recognize and understand the patterns of negativity.

Challenge negative thoughts by questioning their validity. Are they based on facts or assumptions? Reframe them with positive and empowering alternatives. Reminding oneself about an accomplishment earlier in life as evidence can help challenge negative thoughts. Incorporate positive affirmations into your daily routine. Keep repeating statements that reinforce self-belief and challenge the negativity in the subconscious mind.

Vikram and I are making immense progress in our journey. Our stories testify to the transformative power of challenging negative thoughts, embracing growth, and nurturing a mindset that propels individuals beyond worry and into a life of continual expansion.

So, dear reader, if you are struggling in life just like I was, I want to assure you that you can come out of this phase and thrive. It would be best if you decided what you want to do. Craft a vision for your life ahead and seek guidance from mentors and coaches who have walked the path. Stay committed to your vision, and you can surely get on the way to thriving.

Remember, it is never too late. Don't lose hope. You can take inspiration from unlimited stories of people from different walks of life who achieved major success late in their lives.

Embracing the Unwritten Chapters of Your Life

As we navigate the narrative of our lives, let us draw inspiration from those who defied time constraints and societal expectations. Consider the tales of Colonel Sanders, who set up the first KFC restaurant at 62, or Laura Ingalls Wilder, who was 64 when her first book was published. Like many others, these individuals remind us that the story of our lives is an ever-evolving manuscript.

In the same spirit, my dear friend Alifiya Lakdawala is crafting her narrative with her son, both pursuing their educational dreams simultaneously. Alifiya is pursuing a master's in Physiotherapy, while her son Aamir is pursuing a bachelor's degree. Their journey illustrates that there are no predetermined chapters; each day presents an opportunity to script a new page.

As you reflect on the pages of your own life, remember the wise words of Mark Twain: "Twenty years from now, you will be more disappointed by the things you didn't do than by the ones you did." So, let this chapter remind you to throw off the bowlines, sail away from the safe harbor, and embrace the boundless possibilities that await you.

With every turned page and conquered doubt, you become the author of your destiny. The best chapters of your life may be yet to be written, and they await your pen. So, dear reader, with unwavering belief and tenacity, go forth and script the masterpiece that is your life.

Exercise

Reflect on Your Potential:

Take a moment to envision the person you aspire to become. What dreams have you tucked away? What goals have you hesitated to pursue? Allow yourself to dream without limitations.

Set Short-Term Goals: Break down your long-term vision into smaller, manageable goals. What steps can you take in the next month or three months to move toward your vision? Be specific and realistic.

Remember, this exercise is a personal journey. Embrace the process, celebrate small victories, and know that each step forward brings you closer to the life you envision.

If you want me to help you on your journey, kindly click on the link below and fill out the form, and I will get back to you as soon as possible.

https://forms.gle/UyFM1FLjjwZAZwgi6

www.ingramcontent.com/pod-product-compliance
Lightning Source LLC
LaVergne TN
LVHW091112150826
845673LV00002B/785

* 9 7 9 8 8 9 2 3 3 5 8 8 1 *